AF269435

GERMANY

R.L. Van

Big Buddy Books
An Imprint of Abdo Publishing
abdobooks.com

abdobooks.com

Published by Abdo Publishing, a division of ABDO, PO Box 398166, Minneapolis, Minnesota 55439.
Copyright © 2023 by Abdo Consulting Group, Inc. International copyrights reserved in all countries. No part of this book may be reproduced in any form without written permission from the publisher. Big Buddy Books™ is a trademark and logo of Abdo Publishing.

Printed in the United States of America, North Mankato, Minnesota
102022
012023

Design: Emily O'Malley, Mighty Media, Inc.
Production: Mighty Media, Inc.
Editor: Jessica Rusick
Cover Photograph: canadastock/Shutterstock Images
Interior Photographs: Alexandros Michailidis/Shutterstock Images, p. 23; canadastock/Shutterstock Images, p. 6 (middle); dugdax/Shutterstock Images, p. 28 (top); emperorcosar/Shutterstock Images, p. 25; Everett Collection/Shutterstock Images, pp. 11, 28 (bottom); Filip Bjorkman/Shutterstock Images, p. 7 (map); Finn stock/Shutterstock Images, p. 6 (top); FooTToo/Shutterstock Images, p. 26 (right); industryviews/Shutterstock Images, p. 17; Joyja_Lee/Shutterstock Images, p. 27 (bottom); lukulo/iStockphoto, pp. 5 (compass), 7 (compass); Maryna Pleshkun/Shutterstock Images, p. 30 (currency); Michael Mantke/Shutterstock Images, p. 15; o.Ang./Wikimedia Commons, p. 29 (bottom); Pani Garmyder/Shutterstock Images, p. 27 (top left); Pyty/Shutterstock Images, p. 5 (map); Ritu Manoj Jethani/Shutterstock Images, p. 27 (top right); SteffenWalter/Shutterstock Images, p. 19; Travel Faery/Shutterstock Images, p. 6 (bottom); Utah/Shutterstock Images, p. 30 (flag); Viktoriia Adamchuk/Shutterstock Images, p. 26 (left); Vladislav Gajic/Shutterstock Images, p. 13; Wikimedia Commons, pp. 9, 21, 29 (top)
Design Elements: Mighty Media, Inc.
Country population and area figures taken from the CIA World Factbook

Library of Congress Control Number: 2022940530

Publisher's Cataloging-in-Publication Data
Names: Van, R.L., author.
Title: Germany / by R.L. Van
Description: Minneapolis, Minnesota : Abdo Publishing, 2023 | Series: Countries | Includes online resources and index.
Identifiers: ISBN 9781532199615 (lib. bdg.) | ISBN 9781098274818 (ebook)
Subjects: LCSH: Germany--Juvenile literature. | Europe--Juvenile literature. | Germany--History--Juvenile literature. | Geography--Juvenile literature.
Classification: DDC 943--dc23

CONTENTS

PASSPORT TO GERMANY

Germany is a country in central Europe. It has 16 states. It is bordered by two seas. More than 84 million people live there.

WHERE IS GERMANY?
N
W E
S
Denmark
Baltic Sea
North Sea
The Netherlands
Poland
GERMANY
Belgium
Czech Republic
Luxembourg
France
Switzerland
Austria

IMPORTANT CITIES

Berlin is Germany's **capital** and largest city. It was founded in the 1200s. Today, Berlin is a center for business and the arts.

Hamburg is Germany's second-largest city. It is a major port city. It is known for its culture and entertainment.

Munich is Germany's third-largest city. It is known for its festivals and traditional foods.

SAY IT

Berlin
ber-LIHN

Hamburg
HAHM-boorg

Munich
MYOO-nick

DID YOU KNOW?

Hamburg has 2,500 bridges. This is more than any other city in Europe.

GERMANY IN HISTORY

Around the year 500, tribes in present-day Germany were **united** under the Franks. In the 800s, the Frankish **Empire** ended.

German states used to have their own rulers. In the 1800s, many German states were united into the German Empire.

The Franks were a group
of people from several
West Germanic tribes.

9

Germany lost **World War I** in 1918. In 1933, Adolf Hitler and the **Nazi** Party took control. They began the **Holocaust**. Hitler tried to take over other countries. This led to **World War II**.

In 1945, Germany lost the war. It was split into East and West Germany. The country **united** again in 1990.

Adolf Hitler (*standing*) killed or jailed people who stood against him or the Nazi Party.

AN IMPORTANT SYMBOL

Germany adopted its flag after **World War I** and again following **World War II**. Its colors stand for German **unity** and freedom.

Germany is a **federal republic**. Parliament makes laws. The president is head of state. The chancellor is head of government.

The German flag
was first created
in the 1800s.
DEM DEUTSCHEN VOLKE

ACROSS THE LAND

Germany has coasts and valleys. Its mountain ranges include the Bavarian Alps and the Black Forest. Quail, hares, boars, chamois, and many other animals live in Germany. Cornflower, edelweiss, and spruce trees grow there.

SAY IT

Chamois
SHAM-ee

The Black Forest covers
2,320 square miles (6,009 sq km).

EARNING A LIVING

Some Germans work in factories. They make cars, steel, and chemicals. Others have service jobs in sales and health care.

Germany has many **natural resources**. Coal and salt are mined there. Farmers produce grains, potatoes, milk, and pork.

Laws prevent overworking in Germany. Germans cannot work more than 48 hours per week.

LIFE IN GERMANY

Traditional German foods include sauerkraut and sausages. People drink coffee, beer, and wine. Many Germans enjoy soccer, handball, basketball, and tennis. Germany is also known for its festivals.

Almabtrieb is a festival celebrated in Germany. It marks the end of the livestock grazing season in the Alps.

FAMOUS FACES

Steffi Graf was born in Brühl, Germany. During the 1980s and 1990s, she won many tennis tournaments and an Olympic gold medal. She joined the Tennis Hall of Fame in 2004. Today, Graf is known for her charity work.

Steffi Graf (*right*) is married to fellow tennis legend Andre Agassi (*left*).

Angela Merkel was born in Hamburg. She grew up in East Germany before the country was **reunited**. In 2005, she became the first woman chancellor of Germany. She held the position for 16 years before stepping down in 2021.

Angela Merkel supported international cooperation while chancellor of Germany.

A GREAT COUNTRY

Germany is known for its beautiful land and unique culture. The people and places of Germany help make the world a more interesting place.

Germany is home to thousands of ancient castles, such as the Neuschwanstein Castle in the Bavarian Alps.

TOUR BOOK

PLAY

Go skiing in the Bavarian Alps! These mountains are home to Germany's highest peak, Zugspitze.

CELEBRATE

Experience parades, rides, music, and traditional foods at Oktoberfest in Munich.

LEARN

Visit some of Germany's many museums, such as the Natural History Museum in Berlin.

SEE

Miniatur Wunderland in Hamburg is the world's largest model railway. It has miniatures of scenes from around the world.

EXPLORE

Visit the many towns along the Fairy Tale Route. Stop for fairy-tale plays, puppet shows, festivals, and more.

TIMELINE

1517

German monk Martin Luther began the Reformation, which led to the creation of the Lutheran Church.

1871

Germany **united** as the German **Empire** after the Franco-Prussian War.

1685

Famous **composer** Johann Sebastian Bach was born.

1989

People began to tear down the Berlin Wall, which had divided Berlin since 1961.

2010

The 200th Oktoberfest took place in Munich. The first one was held after a royal wedding in 1810.

1939

World War II began. By the end of the war, **Nazis** had killed millions of people. This included about 6 million Jewish people as part of the **Holocaust**.

GERMANY
UP CLOSE

Official Name
Bundesrepublik Deutschland (Federal Republic of Germany)

Flag

Population
84,316,622 (2022 est.)
18th-most-populated country

Total Area
137,847 square miles (357,022 sq km)
63rd-largest country

Official Language
German

Capital
Berlin

Currency
Euro

Form of Government
Federal parliamentary republic

National Anthem
Third stanza of "Deutschlandlied" ("Song of Germany")

GLOSSARY

capital—a city where government leaders meet.

composer—a person who writes music.

empire—a large group of states or countries under one ruler called an emperor or empress.

federal republic—a form of government in which the people choose the leader. The central government and the individual states share power.

Holocaust—the mass murder of Jewish people by the Nazis of Germany between 1941 and 1945.

natural resources—useful and valuable supplies from nature.

Nazi—a member of the National Socialist German Workers Party.

philosopher—a thinker who studies questions about life, right and wrong, meaning, and more.

united—joined together for purpose or action. Unity is the state of being joined together. To reunite is to join together again.

World War I—a war fought in Europe from 1914 to 1918.

World War II—a war fought in Europe, Asia, and Africa from 1939 to 1945.

ONLINE RESOURCES

To learn more about Germany, please visit **abdobooklinks.com** or scan this QR code. These links are routinely monitored and updated to provide the most current information available.

INDEX